The

5 Habits

of Highly
Successful
Business People

Lee Thomas

Printed in the United States of America
by Lightning Source, Inc.

ISBN 978-0-9837470-5-5
Library of Congress Control Number 2014900005

Published 2014 by BookCrafters, Parker, Colorado.
SAN-859-6352, BookCrafters@comcast.net

Copies of this book may be ordered from
www.bookcrafters.net
and other online bookstores.

TABLE OF CONTENTS

FOREWORD

Business is a Great Game. Albeit, a very serious game, it has "players," strategies, rules/boundaries, basic principles, techniques, and "measurement." Attracting the right players, having the right "game plan," making the right game decisions, overcoming the competition, and enjoying the rewards of success are all a part of the Great Game of Business.

To succeed in the "Great Game of Business," I believe there are ways to gain the "talent" to learn how to play and be successful as a player. To that extent, I have written this book. I truly believe that learning, practicing, and sharing the information presented in this book will lead to sustainable business success.

INTRODUCTION

Over the past several years of meeting with clients and giving presentations, I am often asked, "What are your secrets to success?" Always, I would give an answer based on whatever came to my mind at the time. Eventually, I thought that possibly there was a "formula" for business success. Soon, I began to reflect on my career of 40 years of multiple business ownership. I wrote down the successes, and what lead to those successes. Also, and maybe more importantly, I wrote down the missteps, and what lead to them. Having been involved in 10 different industries or market sectors, I would always seek out the people who were successful. I believe in not re-inventing the wheel, but in enhancing what has already been invented. I would detail the reasons for their successes, and when possible note the reasons for their missteps. In addition, I made a habit of reading about successful businesses and the leaders of those businesses. As I examined the information that I had written down, a pattern began to evolve. From the pattern, I have compiled "The Five Habits of Highly Successful Business People." Truly, I believe that every person that will learn these five habits, practice them, and possibly share them with others, will significantly increase the probability of their business success.

CHAPTER ONE

It is always the simple that produces the marvelous.

Definition of Terms

It is important that we define some of the terms used in the title of this book. In doing, so, hopefully you, the reader, and I, will be "on the same page" as we proceed.

HABIT

A Habit is an action that one does repeatedly. It can be a negative or positive action. Examples of negative actions (actions that produce negative effects to our wellbeing) are biting our fingernails, smoking, procrastinating, over eating, etc. Get the picture? These are actions that will be counterproductive to our health, our wellbeing, and our attainment of life or business success.

On the other hand, habits can be positive actions (actions that produce positive effects to our wellbeing). Examples of positive actions are brushing our teeth (remember I was a Dentist), exercising regularly, reading uplifting literature, etc. These are actions that will be an enhancement to our health, or wellbeing, and our attainment of life or business success.

SUCCESS

Countless books, articles, and presentations have been written and produced that examine the concept of success. Almost everyone would agree that "success" is a process, not an "end-point." Likewise, most everyone would like "to be successful." So, given these two paradigms, what is your "vision of success?" Since success is a "path," not a destination, having a "vision of success" or clear understanding of what success means to you, will help you achieve it. It also will help you to determine and clarify your goals. You cannot take the right path if you do not recognize which is the right path. "Success in business" should be clearly defined, and consistent with the other components of your life, and your core values. As you know (or will find out), being in business effects virtually every aspect of your life.

I would encourage you to take a few moments to consider your "vision of success" in the following areas: (Write down your thoughts)

ECONOMIC_____

BUSINESS_____

FAMILY_____

LIFESTYLE_____

HEALTH_____

COMMUNITY_____

and

SPIRITUAL_____

Having done this exercise, you now have YOUR working definition of Success, and are in a position to attain it.

BUSINESS PEOPLE

The FIVE HABITS OF HIGHLY SUCCESSFUL BUSINESS PEOPLE pertain to both business owners and people who are engaged in business commerce, although they may not be a business owner. These habits work for both.

CHAPTER TWO

USE COMMON SENSE

Life is really very simple,
but we insist on making it complicated"
— Confucius

This is Habit number one. As you read through this book, you will come to realize that most of the information in it is not new to you. This is "stuff" that you already know. Success in business is not a matter of quantum physics or empirical discoveries. In my undergraduate education, I found things like Calculus, Differential Equations, and Fluid Dynamics much more intellectually challenging than attaining sustainable business success. However, Calculus and Differential Equations never were instrumental in my personal or business success. It was mastering things much less complex and complicated. Truly,

9

sustainable success is derived from the practice of certain habits.

Habit number one is to "use common sense." As you read this, you probably think, "well of course." It would almost seem self-evident, that we should use common sense. As I reviewed my career and observed other successful people, it became obvious to me, that not always did I use common sense, and to my astonishment, I found others did not also.

We are not born with common sense. We are born with intellectual capability. Essentially, this is what differentiates human beings for all of the other animals on the planet. Common sense is something that is learned over a period of time. It is a continuing process. A couple of my favorite quotes are: "Most good decisions come from experience, and most experience comes from making bad decisions," and "Experience is something you don't get until just after you need it."

As I reflected on my career, especially my missteps and the missteps of others, I found to my surprise examples where I and others had not used common sense in making decisions. Often I had made "the same mistake" twice or even more than twice. Sometimes ego gets in the way of common sense. A real corollary to using common sense is to not make the same mistake or misstep twice (let alone three or four times). In making important decisions, determine what your common sense (intuition) tells you, and set aside your ego.

I recently read a quote from a contemporary NBA superstar commenting on his experience. "No book can really teach you about life. The best teacher of life is experience, and when you experience things it's how you handle them the next time they come upon you." Some additional thoughts on common sense that I like are:

> *"The three great essentials to achieve anything*
> *worthwhile are, first, hard work; second,*
> *stick-to-itiveness; third, common sense."*
> — Thomas A. Edison

Another,

> *"It is the obvious which is so difficult to see most of the*
> *time. People say 'It's as plain as the nose on your face.'*
> *But how much of the nose on your face can you see,*
> *unless someone holds a mirror up to you?"*
> — Isaac Asimov, *I, Robot*

And

> *"Common sense is seeing things as they are;*
> *and doing things as they ought to be."*
> — Harriet Beecher Stowe

I believe these help to establish the importance and relevance of using common sense.

Sometimes you have to exercise a little patience when making important decisions to give common sense the opportunity to rise to your conscious level. So, when making important decisions, don't be in a hurry. Exercise "prudent patience," which is not to be confused with compliancy or procrastination.

When you employ the habit of using common sense in making decisions, you will be amazed at the number of good decisions you make, and the missteps that you avoid.

CHAPTER THREE

Thoroughly Understand & Employ Correct Business Principles

*The two most important days of your life
are the day when you are born, and the day
when you find out why.*

This is Habit number two. To do this, we must first identify correct business principles. Then we have to understand them. Once this is accomplished, we must employ them correctly.

So, what are correct business principles? They are like the "core values" in our personal lives. They are time tested, and do not vary over time or circumstances. The have been proven by experience and outcome to be true. Sometimes they are difficult to identify, but like core values which have been laid down over the ages by prophets, sages and persons of "great enlightenment," correct business principles can be identified. One has to examine business literature, the writings of proven successful business people, and "best business practices" to find them.

I believe there are "overarching" correct business principles and specific business principles. First we will identify three "overarching" correct business principles.

The first is Passion.

While giving a presentation one time and expounding on the virtue of Passion, an attendee raised his hand and asked if I have been passionate about being a Dentist. Honestly, the question took me aback for a moment, and I had to admit that I was not. I had enjoyed becoming a Dentist and being one. But, I was not passionate about Dentistry. He then followed that up by asking if I was passionate about Childcare, knowing that I had owned multiple childcare centers. Again, I had to answer that I was not. I enjoyed the experience, but certainly I was not "passionate" about it. Then, if by inspiration, it occurred to me that what I was passionate about was small BUSINESS. I believe that small business is the backbone of our country, its economy and in part its culture. I am passionate about the entire experience of "being in business;" starting or acquiring, building, and exiting successfully. So, I would suggest that one needs to be passionate about what they are doing, what they are "about." The main reason for having passion is that it will sustain you through the difficult times, and there will be difficult times. Without passion, one will quit, because like Steve Jobs says, "they are sane."

The second overarching principle is Perseverance.

This book does not have enough pages for me to share with you the many challenges, missteps, and disappointments I have had in my adventures as a multiple business owner. I can state unequivocally, that it has been perseverance that has allowed to me to recover or come out "whole" after the experience. This correct business principal has been, for me, a major reason for the sustainable business success I have enjoyed. Perseverance requires that you have confidence in yourself and a well-developed sense of personal self-esteem. It must be accompanied by a sure knowledge of your "True North." It, like Common Sense, is something that comes over a period of time. False or "faked" Perseverance derived from arrogance will not sustain one to achieving sustainable business success.

The third overarching principle is Attitude.

Like success, the concept of Attitude has been the subject of many books, articles, and presentations. Years ago, a very popular movement was to teach techniques to gain a "Positive Mental Attitude" (PMA). One could buy books, read magazines, and attend rallies and speakers giving the techniques to acquire or manifest "Positive Mental Attitude." Certainly there is nothing wrong with having a positive mental attitude. However, it was my experience that I had to continually read or attend seminars to sustain my positive attitude. It seemed to me to be something that required continual external input and reinforcement. Over a period of years of studying the topic of attitude, I discovered that a better approach was to have the "Correct Attitude." The "Correct Attitude" was a product of identifying one's true core values ("True North"), and employing them in every aspect of business and personal life. The power of "The Correct Attitude" is the single most important principle I have found to sustainable business success.

Now, on to the Correct Business Principles.

Business is like the human body. As the human body has different organs and systems which must work in harmony, so does a business. No single organ or system works independently of the others. This is also true of a business.

To demonstrate the concept of the Habit: "Understand Thoroughly, & and Employ Correct Business Principles," let's consider four business "organs/ systems:" Financial, Marketing, Sales, and Personnel. Certainly, there are other "organs/systems" in business, but these are the major ones, and serve as good examples of this Habit.

Here are some (not all inclusive) examples of Correct Principles that apply to the **Financial** "organ/system" of business:

Cash is the life blood of a business.

In the body, when there is insufficient blood, the body begins to "shut down," it goes into shock. If not replenished to an acceptable level the body dies. The same is true of a business. When cash is inadequate it goes into "shock." Poor decisions result. Panic sets in, and the business becomes very vulnerable to employing spurious business practices, ultimately leading to business death (out of business).

Know the Key Performance Indicators (KPI) of your business.

It is essential that the business owner identifies the KPI of his/her business. These are the key line items on the Profit & Loss, Balance Sheet, and other financial reports of the business. The KPI of a business is like the vital signs of the body, and it is important to monitor them to be sure all organs/systems are functioning properly.

Have a good, competent "professional team" to assist you in your business.

Of course, as this relates to financial, this would be a competent Accountant, CPA, Bookkeeper, and Financial Services advisor. The business owner cannot be an expert in all areas of business, and having and employing competent professionals in the areas outside of the business owner's core competencies is a must.

Here are <u>some</u> (not all inclusive) examples of Correct Principles that apply to the **Marketing** "organ/system" of business:

Have AND implement an effective Marketing Strategy.

Marketing is the action of making potential customers aware of the business's products and services. It is not to be confused with sales.

An effective Marketing Strategy must be implemented consistently and continually.

Too often, business owners only think about marketing when sales are down. It, like food for the body, must be employed continually to sustain the business's wellbeing and health.

Here are <u>some</u> (not all inclusive) examples of Correct Principles that apply to the **Sales** "organ/system" of business:

The single most important thing that a business must have is Sale(s).

I have asked many, many business people what the single most important thing that a business must have. Over 95% of the responses have been things such as a business plan, adequate capital, mission statement, personnel, etc. All of these are important, but they are not the single most important thing that a business must have. Without sale(s), a business is not a business it is a hobby. This is true even if the business is a "not for profit" business entity.

People buy from people that they know, like and trust.

Remember, I stated that operating a business successfully is not quantum mechanics or complicated. Yes, this is obvious, but it is critical that this principle is employed continually, and sustained by proper techniques (in the next chapter).

Sell OUTCOMES.

Too often, we focus on the features and benefits of the products and services that our business provides. The consumer is really only interested in "what is in it for me" (WIIFM). As a Dentist, my patients were not interested in how I made the crown, bridge or did the root canal. They really just wanted to know that it would not hurt, was done properly, and would contribute to their good oral health.

Effective communication is paramount to an effective relationship.

It begins with effective listening. The person asking the questions controls the conversation. Always listen first to the person with whom you are having a conversation with, and want to develop a quality relationship. Take genuine interest in them. Ask questions that begin with who, what, why, when, where, and how. You will be surprised how well the conversation proceeds. Most importantly, the other person will often comment on the positive or "great" conversation you have had with them.

Here are some (not all inclusive) examples of Correct Principles that apply to the **Personnel** "organ/system" of business:

People are the heart of the business.

As a business owner, it is important that we recognize the importance of the fact that our people are the heart of our business, and just like we would for our body, practice techniques (in the next chapter) to have good "heart health" in our business.

Treat your employees the way you want them to treat your customers.

Essentially this is the practice of the "golden rule."

Hire for attitude and train for skills.

Certainly, there are certain basic skills that a new employee must possess when we consider hiring them. This is especially true in technical areas, Dentists, Hygienists, Nurses, Acupuncturists, Plumbers, etc. However, I found that it is very difficult to "train attitude" in a person. It is extremely important to look beyond the basic skills to determine if the new hire you are considering has the correct attitude. Will they fit in the culture of your business? Is their attitude congruent with yours and the culture of the business?

You must practice effective delegation.

Effective delegation is both an art and a

science. To be effective as a business owner, a person must master this art and science. The underlying principle is to learn to be a "cultivator or gardener" of people.

Manage "things," and lead people.

Managing people is a concept from the now irrelevant industrial age. Leading people is critical to the sustained success of a business. It is facilitated, in part, by effective delegation.

Here are some more (not all inclusive) examples of Correct Principles that apply to **other** "organ/system" of business:

Do a lot of small, but important things consistently and correctly.

True, sustainable success is often found in "the details" and implementing consistently.

Mistakes are for learning, they are good!

Try not to make them twice.

If it sounds too good to be true, avoid it.

True, sustainable success only comes over a period of time. There are very few exceptions.

This, for an entrepreneur is possibly one of the hardest principles to adhere to.

In every new situation, get well informed, ask; who, what, when, why, where and how.
Knowledge is power which is necessary to effect positive change.

Have rules to "your game," and make sure everyone plays by the rules.

If you don't have rules you will have chaos. It is your business, so make your rules, and make sure they are consistent with your core values.

Have options in all aspects of your business.

Without options we can become "boxed in" and "trapped." This leads to fear which leads to a shutdown of good decision making.

Good relationships are golden.

Start and keep a good contact database. It is invaluable to sustained business success. Remember, quality relationships require maintenance.

Base your business on a firm foundation (principles).

You can learn the "techniques," and they will come and go (this is the subject of the next chapter).

Have both long term and short term vision.

In other words, your long term vision is where you are going with the business. The short term vision is being aware of the trends that will affect your business. You always want to be in front of the curve regarding short term vision. It is concerned with the "how" of getting there.

Practice "expedient patience."

Rome was not built in a day, and neither will your business. "Expedient Patience" should not be confused with being complacent or neglect. It is practicing disciplined perseverance.

Never, never make "snap," uninformed or emotional decisions.

There is always time, and never be pressured into a decision.

As we come to the conclusion of this chapter, I hope you are beginning to see the logic in the application of the Five Habits. It is like a funnel. It starts with a broader perspective and it continually narrows to a methodology of operating a business. As the funnel narrows, we now move to considering the techniques that support the Correct Business Principles we have learned and employ.

CHAPTER FOUR

Don't judge each day by the harvest you reap
but by the seeds that you plant.

Utilize Techniques that Support
Correct Business Principles

This is Habit number three.

Techniques are often mistaken for business principles. But, Techniques are time sensitive, unlike Correct Business Principles, which are not time sensitive. Their (techniques) effectiveness can be transient, and will vary over time.

An example of this is that about 35 years ago I was placing a small display advertisement in the metropolitan Denver telephone directory, the "yellow pages." At that time, it was the only telephone directory for the Denver area. The ad was for my, at the time, two childcare centers. As I talked with the representative, I asked him if I could also place a similar ad for my dental office. He responded that he did not know, since that had never been done before in Denver or Colorado. He would check with his supervisor. A few days later, he called me to say that his supervisor had given him the OK to place a dental ad. We took the same ad with a picture of a cute little boy, and changed the name from "Thomas Learning Centers," to "Family Dental Care," L. E. Thomas, DMD, and into the directory it went. This was in the fall of the year. In the spring of the following year, the directory came out. Our telephone at the dental office really began to ring with new patient inquiries. My staff thought that I was the "marketing guru" of Denver, and I even thought that I was the marketing genius of Dentistry. Fast forward to the present time. An ad in the "yellow pages," of which now there are many, let alone an 1/8 of a page ad, would be completely ineffective. This is an example of how techniques and their effectiveness change over time. The principle would be the same: The business must have an effective marketing program, but the technique to support that principle has certainly changed.

Now let us consider some Techniques that support the Correct Business Principles we have identified in the previous chapter. Namely, the four "organs/ systems" of a business: Financial, Marketing, Sales, and Personnel. Certainly, there other "organs/ systems" in business, but these are the major ones, and serve as good examples of this Habit.

Here are some (not all inclusive) examples of

Techniques that apply to the **Financial** "organ/system" of business: Cash related techniques.

Have multiple lines of Credit.

Having access to cash when it is needed is paramount to the health of a business. Equally important, is having more than one source as a line of credit. I had a client who had only one bank source as a line of credit. When their bank decided to "close" their line of credit, it was disastrous for them. They were a seasonal type of business. The bank closed their line of credit just as their peak season was in progress. They could not acquire the supplies they required and had a difficult time meeting payroll and other obligations. Try as they may, finding an alternative bank line of credit was difficult during their peak season, and it was almost the end of their business. So, it is important to have a least two bank lines of business credit. Certainly, it should go without saying, judicious use of the funds is extremely important, and a definite plan for repayment must be in place.

Have alternate sources of operating capital and expansion capital.

Since cash is the life blood of a business, not only in terms of operations, but also in terms of capital for expansion, it is imperative to have alternative sources in place. The technique is to be proactive in securing possible sources. This could include companies the factor invoices and/or discount (purchase) invoices. Another source would be private short term investors, which could be family members or business associates. The point is to have in place BEFORE the need, sources of cash.

Do cash flow projections.

This, again, is being proactive. Doing quarterly cash flow projections or forecasts prevents having "cash crunches" before they happen.

Utilize Source and Use of cash reports.

This type of report, done usually on a monthly basis demonstrates to the business owner where the money came from and exactly where it went. If, as a business owner, you are not aware of this, you are not in control of your business.

Have in place a budget.

Compare the financial results of your business to the budgets you have proactively established. Utilizing this technique also helps the business owner in establishing realistic budgets, AND in developing the discipline to actually follow budgets.

Implement proven Accounts Receivable and Accounts Payable policies and procedures.

Constant, methodical monitoring of A/R and A/P is critical to a good cash management program. A specific person should be in charge of both monitoring and implementing the A/R and A/P policies. Always remember that the older Accounts Receivable are the harder they are to collect.

Have a regularly scheduled meeting with the appropriate professional on the "professional team."

This meeting should produce results that expedite the business owner's proactive initiatives regarding the financial management of the business, not just cash management.

Here are some (not all inclusive) examples of Techniques that apply to the **Marketing** "organ/system" of business:

"Hoping" is not an effective marketing technique.

Too often people think they have an effective marketing technique because they have a website, or they have a marketing plan which has never been initiated.. They assume or "hope" that "things will happen." What will happen is virtually nothing. Tangible, measureable initiatives must be implemented.

All messaging must about "WIIFM," What's In It For Me from the potential customer's perspective.

Features and benefits of provided products or services are used to support the perspective of "WIIFM." Customers are really mainly interested in what the product or service will do for them. They are interested in "OUTCOMES" that will be of a benefit to them.

Be creative in your marketing.

Do not try to emulate the "Big Guys" or your competition. A small business cannot economically compete with the "Big Guys," and if someone else has already done it, it is now "stale."

Focus on building a quality network.

Effective marketing focuses on building a quality network, NOT on networking. Too often business people confuse the two. Most networking boils down to attending events, being "stabbed and stabbing" others with business cards to see how many can be accumulated during the event. Focus on finding business people with which to build a quality, mutually beneficial network, the purpose of which is to enhance each other's business enterprise. I had a client that bragged that she had attended an event and collected 25 business cards. I suggested that she could have just gone to the telephone book and accomplished the same thing. Obviously it is about "quality" not "quantity."

Understand the true purpose of the Internet as related to Marketing.

The purpose of internet marketing is to gain awareness of the business's products and services. Most generally it is not to make a sale, with the exceptions being online stores such as Amazon, etc. If you choose to have an online store presence, that requires a modified approach to internet marketing. SEO (search engine optimization) and SMO (search engine marketing optimization) are only techniques to provide "new revenue opportunities," or "NRO." "NROs" are essentially, warm or qualified leads. What is important is that the "NROs" or warm leads are converted into sales.

Here are some (not all inclusive) examples of Techniques that apply to the **Sales** "organ/system" of business:

Make it easy for the potential customer to buy.

This technique embodies such things as providing competitive financing, liberal, but realistic terms, easy & timely access to the products or services, easy access and parking if in a brick and mortar location, etc.

Utilization of an effective sales software program and process.

Using an effective computer supported sales program and process is essential to sustainable sales production. Setting realistic daily, weekly and quarterly objective which are diligently measured on a routine basis is paramount. An effective such program we developed called the "Rapid Results Sales Program" and is detailed in the appendix.

Always present "outcomes" to customers.

As previously mentioned, customers are interested basically in what is in it for them. The features and benefits of any given product or service only support the outcomes that a customer wants and expects to derive from the product or service.

Listen carefully and sincerely.

An old saying is, "people don't care how much you know, but how much your care." Always practice "relationship selling," namely build quality relationships, because people buy from people they know, like and trust.

Here are some (not all inclusive) examples of Techniques that apply to the **Personnel** "organ/system" of business:

Practice Management By Walking Around, "MBWA."

Catch people doing things right. Make notes on sticky notes and put them in each person's personnel file. When time to evaluate a person use the accumulated sticky notes to provide a clear picture of the individual.

Utilize Effective Delegation.

Using the techniques embodied in Effective Delegation is critical to achieving a desired culture in an enterprise, motivating the people in an enterprise, and getting the owner/operator off of "the treadmill." The details of how to implement Effective Delegation are given in the appendix.

Use Position Descriptions as your "KPI."

Position Descriptions determine the Key Performance Indicators (KPI) for every position in the business enterprise. When evaluating the performance of an employee these indicators are used to monitor and measure the degree of successful or anticipated performance.

Utilize "Relationship Checkups."

As previously mentioned, employee reviews are actually counterproductive. They have the subtle tendency of elevating the supervisor over the employee. In the modern world of enlightened business practices, this is not acceptable. An employee is a vital "contributor" to the welfare and wellbeing of the business enterprise, and should be treated as such. Using the "Relationship Checkup" in place of the employee review system greatly contributes to the positive culture, positive morale, and overall productivity of the business enterprise. The protocol and forms for the "Relationship Checkup" are detailed in the appendix.

NOTE: Forms can be ordered by contacting the author at lee@myIBV.com or info@integritybusinesssolutions. com.

By this time, I hope that it is evident how each Habit builds upon another. Since there are other Correct Business Principles that apply to a business, it is important that when they are identified and employed, the appropriate techniques be identified to support each them also. As you now see the pattern, the "funnel" is getting narrower and narrower, and we move to the next Habit, and that is to Take Action.

CHAPTER FIVE

*I can't change the direction of the wind, but I can
adjust my sails to always reach my destination.*

Take Action

This is the fourth Habit: Take Action.

As with much of what has already been presented,
this seems obvious and very simple. It is surprising how
many people, however find this Habit difficult. Often
business owners "strategize and plan" way too much.
Strategizing and planning is important, but once done,
and it should be done with a limit on the time to do it,
"get up, get out, and do it!"

**Sometimes fear can be the reason that a business
owner or business person hesitates or does not take
action. Do not let fear stop you.**

In any endeavor of importance in the life experience, Fear is a natural component of that experience. Consider, if you will, marriage, childbirth, dental or medical treatments, and major purchases (home, car, etc.). They all have a certain amount of fear and/or anxiety associated with them. The same is true for going into business, being in business, and making business decisions.

You can anticipate the "Fear Factor" to increase the closer you get to having to make a definitive decision, or take the steps necessary to move your business forward. Therefore, the question becomes will Fear be a motivator, causing you to be careful, cautious, and do appropriate due diligence, and then take ACTION? Or, will Fear be an inhibitor, paralyzing or stopping you from making appropriate decisions that could enhance your business and your life?

If you choose to let Fear be an inhibitor, you choose to allow Fear to control your destiny. You abdicate the responsibility for your life to it. Indeed, your destiny will never reach its full potential, and your life experience will only manifest a limited or small degree of what it could be.

How can you make Fear work in your favor, i.e., be your motivator? The answer is KNOWLEDGE. When you strive to acquire a full spectrum of knowledge on any life endeavor, the paralyzing attributes of Fear are reduced and even eliminated. Knowledge means understanding correct principles, applying appropriate techniques, and taking action, followed by appropriate measurement.

Knowledge is power. It becomes the power to effect change, and to create positive change in your life. Change, in life, is inevitable, and it can be the seed for growth. But, growth is optional, and it is up to you. If you use knowledge to make Fear "your motivator," it becomes the engine for your positive growth. With knowledge, you significantly increase the probability of success in life. You will reach your business's and your life's full potential. The choice is yours.

Inaction breads doubt and fear. Action breeds confidence and courage. If you want to conquer fear, stop ruminating or just thinking and thinking. Go out and take action.

I think a quote from the late Steve Jobs is appropriate:

"The benefit of death is you know not to waste life living someone else's choices. Don't let the noise of others' opinions drown out your own inner voice. And, most important, have the courage to follow your heart and intuition."

Business Plans do not work; Business Strategize/ Campaigns do.

All too often a great deal of time, energy, and resources are put into developing the right business plan. Except for those instances that one is required for a lender or investor, I believe they are a waste of time. Most business plans are rarely looked at after they have been completed and submitted to the appropriate third party. In reading the history of many of the successful businesses in America, none of them started with a formal business plan. An example is Hewlett Packard. When they started in a garage in Palo Alto California, the avowed plan of Bill Hewlett and David Packard was to provide current technology to customers. Their first product was an electronic bowling alley foul line monitor which did not sell well. That was followed by an automatic toilet flushing mechanism, which also did not sell well. Other products were made for the agricultural sector which did not sell. They developed the 200A test instrument, and finally they had product sales. One of the company's earliest customers was Walt Disney Productions, which bought eight Model 200B oscillators (at $71.50 each) for use in certifying the "Fantasound" surround sound systems installed in theaters for the movie Fantasia.

Henry J. Heinz (founder of H.J. Heinz, Catsup) went bankrupt several times, once in an ice company venture and another in a packing food stuffs venture with his friend Clarence Noble.

The largest dot com failure was a company known as Web Van. It had a business plan developed by very astute business people, raised large amounts of capital, and at one time had a Wall Street value in the billions. It went out of business in a relatively short time. I believe that one of the major reasons was that "upper management" was so sure of their "business plan" that they would not listen to "the people on the street." They were not flexible until it was too late.

It is better to do a Business "Strategy or Campaign." This is like a mini business plan. It is a three-to-four month plan of exactly what you are going to accomplish the goals and objectives you have outlined for the business. Doing a business strategy/campaign allows (forces) the business owner to be flexible.

The action taken must be purposeful and targeted.

When one goes duck hunting, it is probably appropriate to use a shotgun. In business, using the "shotgun approach" is sure business suicide. Once the business strategy/campaign has been developed, it must be implemented in a focused or targeted manner. Using this technique allows the business owner to implement the next of the Five Habits, which is Measurement or Accountability. If the action or initiative is too broad and unfocused it is difficult to measure, and the results are often disappointing.

Know when to "fold ém.

In the Great Game of Business, I am reminded that it is like a game of poker. To get into the game, the player has to "ante up." That means he/she puts money in the pot which gives him/her the opportunity to play. This is the case in business. The capital involved in starting or acquiring a business is essentially the "ante" that allows a person to play the Great Game of Business. Once in the game, success is dependent upon a number of factors; the skill and knowledge of the player, the skill of the other players (the competition), and the cards that are dealt. This is exactly the same for the person playing the Great Game of Business. The skill and knowledge of the individual business person, the skill or degree of the competition and the factors external to the business all contribute to the success or lack of success of the business. However, skillful poker players know when to "fold ém." They know when the odds of winning a hand or round are too great against them. This is also true of the person in business. Sometimes it just comes down to the fact that it is best to "fold ém," and be able to come back and play again. All too often emotion, and wishful thinking overwhelm the business owner, and he/she continues way beyond what is the prudent course. This is very unfortunate, because I have seen it demolish marriages and what had been quality relationships.

To take action is to be "proactive." Successful people are proactive. That means that they "act" rather than being "acted upon." To be acted upon removes control of our life from us, and places it with someone or something else. It causes us to make excuses for our circumstances rather than to take responsibility for our circumstances. Taking responsibility for our actions and our circumstances requires a well-developed character ethic. It requires us to understand our "True North," our well established core values. It is a sign of "maturity." There is absolutely no question, that to be successful in business, for that matter, in life, one has to be proactive. Take action!

Doing so, moves us to the final Habit of Highly Successful Business People, that of Measurement or Accountability. This is the narrowest part of the "focus funnel" and helps us manifest all of the Habits that have come before.

CHAPTER SIX

If opportunity doesn't knock, build a door. √

Measure the Right Things (Accountability)

This is Habit number five.

For me, measurement or accountability was probably the hardest Habit to incorporate in my management style. Early in my career, everything was "coming up roses." It seemed that I could not make a mistake. Then, one day I discovered that the young man who was in charge of a new little business I had acquired was putting revenues in his pocket. It became apparent that for every five dollars given to him by customers, two of them went into his pocket. I was shocked. Needless to say, he was dismissed. Immediately, new protocols were put in place to prevent such a thing from happening in the future. It was a lesson learned the "hard way." In fact, as I look back, it seems that many lessons I have learned over the years have been "the hard way." Several years later, I had acquired a small plumbing and heating company. After a couple of years, we had been experiencing great growth and prosperity. We were enjoying an annualized revenue of almost $2,000,000. I hired a new day manager for the business. He had appropriate industry managerial experience, and the staff really liked him. At this point in time, we had a complete in house accounting staff consisting of three bookkeepers and an experienced, full charge accountant. The accounting staff had responsibility for "keeping the books" for all of the dental offices, all of the childcare centers, a home inspection company, and the plumbing and heating company. When hiring the accountant, I had made sure he knew that one of my high priorities was financial accountability.

One day, the accountant came into my office to tell me that something was wrong with the financials of the plumbing and heating company. He said it had to do with a "clearing account" that he had set up. Quite honestly, I did not know what a "clearing account" was, but was impressed that his accountability measures had uncovered a problem. Upon investigation, it was determined that the manager of the plumbing and heating company had set up fake vendors to the company. We had been processing checks to these fake vendors for almost four months. The amount of the embezzlement approached almost $30,000. Needless to say, the manager was dismissed. Had the accountant not put in place accountability (measurement) protocols the loss could have been much more.

I cannot emphasize to strongly the importance of measurement (accountability) not only in the financial areas **but all areas of business**.

Here are some (not all inclusive) examples of Measurement or Accountability that apply to the **Financial** "organ/system" of business:

Know and review regularly your "numbers" your KPI (Key Performance Indicators).

Every business has Key Performance Indicators, and the business owner must be intimately familiar with them. A competent Accountant can help a business owner identify the KPIs. Measuring and monitoring them is critical to effective financial management of the business.

Conduct regular reviews of Performance vs. Budget reviews.

This measurement tool helps the business to stay on track financially.

Do regular cash flow projections.

Doing regular cash flow projections will avoid having unexpected "cash crunches."

Have and review regularly a "source and use of cash report."

This is yet another tool to help the business owner maintain control of the financial aspect of their business. It should be done monthly.

Here are some (not all inclusive) examples of Measurement or Accountability that apply to the **Marketing** "organ/system" of business:

Relate the number of "New Revenue Opportunities" (NRO) to the cost of the marketing initiative.

Too often business owners make the mistake of relating the cost of the marketing initiative to sales. Marketing is the process of gaining customer awareness of the business's products and services. Its main purpose (with some exceptions such as online product sales/services) is to generate "New Revenue Opportunities" (NROs). This is another term for "warm and/ or qualified" leads for the business. The next step is to convert the NRO into a sale. Relate the cost of the marketing initiative per NRO, or lead generated. Then it can be determined if the marketing initiative is cost effective. Of course it is important to identify the dollar value of a sale and relate it in the comparison. Obviously, even if a significant number of NROs are developed and converted into sales, but the sale value is too small, there is a problem. This is covered in the next example of measurement related to sales.

Track the numbers or "metrics" of the business's website and other online activities.

This measurement protocol can easily be performed by a competent website administrator. It, along with all other internet initiatives, should be reviewed on a regular basis.

Be prepared to change marketing initiatives based on the measurement tools that have been put in place.

This, of course, relates back to Habit number four, Take Action. When measurement indicators demonstrate that something is not working, have other options at the ready, and be ready to employ them. Set limits on how long a particular marketing initiative has to demonstrate effectiveness and efficacy.

Here are some (not all inclusive) examples of Measurement or Accountability that apply to the **Sales** "organ/system" of business:

Utilize a software program to track and "analyze" the probability of sales.

Usually, sales are not a "sure thing." There is a probability relative to their consummation. An effective software program should, in addition to maintaining the customer database, be able to analyze the probability of a sale. This is especially important with "high ticket" sales.

Measure the sale(s) results against the direct cost to produce the sale(s).

All too often, the emphasis is on "producing sales." If the cost of producing the sale is more than the value of the sale, it should be obvious that producing mores sales only puts the business deeper in the financial hole. Know the cost of sales at all levels of sales. Do not fall for the illusion that increasing sales will "take care of things." How often I have heard, "we can make it up in volume." That is insanity.

Set weekly sales process objectives and measure performance against the preset objectives.

A very effective process that we have developed called "The Rapid Results Sales Process" is detailed in the appendix of this book. I encourage you to consider incorporating it, or something like it, in your sales process measurement. Set daily, weekly, and quarterly performance and sales goals. Have the discipline to monitor performance, and adjust the goals and/or the performance accordingly.

Here are some (not all inclusive) examples of Measurement or Accountability that apply to the **Personnel** "organ/system" of business:

Practice Management By Walking Around, (MBWA).

This is a technique pioneered and developed by Hewlett Packard. I can remember working in the machine shop, evenings at the Page Mill Road location in Palo Alto when I went back to college to get into dental school. During that nine month time frame, Dave Packard came down to the machine shop and visited with each of the machine operators three times. He was living proof of a person who "walked their talk."

Employing this measurement tool pays great dividends to the business. The business owner sees firsthand what the culture of the business is. It can provide valuable feedback from the employees to enhance the business. It is not a matter of seeing what the employee is "doing wrong," but what he/she is "doing right."

Utilize Position Descriptions as a standard for evaluating performance.

Position descriptions provide the foundation for evaluating the performance of employees, and also establishes the expectations of the employee as to their worth and value to the company.

Forget performance reviews; conduct "Relationship Checkups."

I have always believed that "employee reviews" are counterproductive, even when I was an employee. This is a throwback to the "industrial age" of business management. The objective is to enhance the relationship between the employee and the business. To do this, years ago, I developed the "Relationship Checkup." The protocol and forms are in the appendix of this book. It embodies all of the above mentioned measurement tools. Be walking around and interfacing with the employees, especially to "catch them doing things right," allows the supervisor to collect valuable input. I would have my managers take notes on yellow sticky notes. These notes would have the employees name and date on each of them. They would be put into the employee's personnel folder. Then, at the time of the "Relationship Checkup" the supervisor would open the folder and get a great picture of the employee over a period of time. It was like looking into a folder of butterflies. With the position description in hand, the employee and the supervisor would engage in a relationship checkup. The results have been amazing in enhancing the relationship between the employees and the business, and in improving the culture of the business.

In summary of Habit Five, it is not the "end all, be all," but is merely a continuum of the Habits, that if diligently practiced, assures success of the business person. The results derived from Habit five are carried back to Habits three and four. This insures that the business adjusts and maintains its heading in the direction that the business person and/or owner desires.

CHAPTER SEVEN

*Put your heart, mind, and soul into even your
smallest acts. This is the secret of success.*

Applying the Five Habits

Now, the fun begins. Applying and implementing the
Five Habits should be an enjoyable, albeit, challenging
experience.

The main reason it can be enjoyable, is that while
practicing the Five Habits, positive results will begin
to manifest themselves. This becomes a positive
reinforcement to continue practicing them.

The reason it can be challenging is that not only does
one have to adopt new habits, but often they have a break
or discontinue old ones. In addition to discontinuing old
ones, to be effective, the new habits must be diligently
practiced for a sustained period of time.

It is claimed that it takes about 21 to 28 days to learn a new habit. That doesn't sound like too long a time, but the research also found that people tend to drop out of a new behavior after about 2 weeks if they didn't go out of their way to keep going. But a new study from psychologist Phillippa Lally of University College London found it took an average of 9.5 weeks to get students to incorporate a new habit into their daily lives. Two and a half months! That's a serious chunk of time. Good for us to remember when starting to work with the Five Habits. There's little question that one of the most common mistakes people make with adopting new habits is to get a good behavior started, and then stop reinforcing it too soon. So stay with it!

Adopting new habits initiates change. Change, for many, is a very difficult thing to do. In fact, for most people, change is very uncomfortable. Whenever we initiate change, even a positive one, we activate fear in our emotional brain. Fear can be the great inhibitor to positive change. However, knowledge combats fear, and with the knowledge you have gained about the Five Habits, incorporating the changes in your business life is very possible.

Virtually every day in business life, decisions are required to be made. Some of them are minor and others are major. Consider the Five Habits as a filter or funnel with five levels. For every decision to be made, even the minor ones, first run it past your COMMON SENSE filter, your intuition. That may be all that you have to do, and you can move on to the other activities of the business day.

If it passes the COMMON SENSE filter run it down the funnel to the next filter which is to determine the CORRECT BUSINESS PRINCIPLES that apply to it. Be sure to consider all of the possible CORRECT BUSINESS PRINCIPLES that may apply. It is even helpful when doing this to write them down for future reference. Remember, these are concepts or axioms that stand the test of time.

Once through this filter, your course has become much clearer, and you are ready to go down the funnel to the next filter, TECHNIQUES. Remember, TECHNIQUES are those actions that support the CORRECT BUSINESS PRINCIPLES. Do not confuse them with being principles. Consider all available TECHNIQUES that may support the CORRECT BUSINESS PRINCIPLE, even the ones that may seem "way out" or crazy. From the list of TECHNIQUES, prioritize them as to the ones most likely to succeed down to the ones that are least likely to succeed. Then choose one to three TECHNIQUES to support your CORRECT BUSINESS PRINCIPLE.

Now it is time for ACTION, time to employ the TECHNIQUES. Here again, is where the old nemesis, Fear, raises its head. Just remember, you now have the power of knowledge behind you, and proceed undaunted. Be sure that your ACTION is focused and targeted toward the results you want to achieve. Also, set a definite time frame around your ACTION and anticipated results.

Now move to the last filter in the funnel, MEASUREMENT. Even as you are formulating you ACTION strategy, determine exactly how you will measure the results. Set up your measurement criteria and time frames. This can, arguably, be the most important filter in the entire process. Utilizing this filter will keep your business ship form straying too far off of its course to sustainable success.

From measuring the results of your ACTION, you will either continue with the ACTION, or you may have to move back up the funnel to employ new TECHNIQUES.

In rare cases, it may be evident that what was thought to be a CORRECT BUSINESS PRINCIPLE was, in fact, not one at all. This is rare, and will not happen if you are diligent in defining CORRECT BUSINESS PRINCIPLES. Remember, they do not vary with time, and span the breadth of business activity.

Enjoy the adventures of mastering the FIVE HABITS, and for even greater mastery, share them with others.

CHAPTER EIGHT

Difficulties are opportunities for inner growth.

Getting "Unstuck"
(In Business and Life)

During the journey of life and business there are times that we can get "stuck." It can be something very simple or very complex. Regardless, "stuck is stuck," and it would be nice to have a template or "guide" as to how to get "unstuck." Also, often being "stuck" has a component of Fear or Frustration associated with it. How can one make Fear or Frustration work in their favor? The answer is KNOWLEDGE. When you strive to acquire a full spectrum of knowledge on any life endeavor, the paralyzing attributes of Fear and Frustration are reduced and even eliminated.

Knowledge is power. It becomes the power to

effect change, and to create positive change in your life and business. Change, in life, is inevitable, and it can be the seed for growth. But, growth is optional, and it is up to you. Use knowledge to make Fear and Frustration "your friend," your engine for your positive growth. With knowledge, you significantly increase the probability of success in life and business. You will reach your life's and business's full potential. The choice is yours.

Knowledge in this case is having a simple template or "guide" to becoming unstuck. Here is that guide:

ASSESSMENT

Assessment is the first step in getting unstuck. Since almost always, our personal lives and business lives are integrally connected, self-assessment and business assessment are the starting points.

Self-assessment is the process of, as objectively as possible, determining your "TRUE NORTH." As much as is possible, set aside your emotions, and consider your CORE VALUES and your "WHY" as is related to your personal life. One of the most important traits of the human psychology that differentiates humans from other animals, is that we must have purpose in our lives to be happy, self-actualized and fulfilled. Without purpose, we are a ship without a rudder. Having a vision of success provides clarity as to our life purpose. Consider what your vision of success (life purpose) is in the following areas:

Family
Economic
Business
Lifestyle
Health
Community
Spiritual (does not necessarily mean "religious," but
   it may)

This often takes some extensive, quiet-time reflection. It is critical that it be done, AND written down. Once composed, it will reveal your "TRUE NORTH," i.e. your life's direction. Because your business is most likely "intimately connected" to your personal life, it will factor into becoming "unstuck" in your business. Until you really become clear in your life vision of success (really more than just goals), you will never be able to become completely "unstuck" in your business.

Now, we come to business assessment. This assessment consists of objectively writing down the "state of the business" in the following areas:

Financial (not just accounting/bookkeeping, but knowing "the numbers" – Key Performance Indicators--measuring, etc.)

Marketing
Sales
Personnel related
Systems and processes
Facilities

Personal (management of you time, energy and
   ability to effectively delegate)
Administrative (all the other stuff such as insurance,
   legal, and not covered above.)

STATEMENT OF CURRENT CONDITION

Based on the above assessments, you can now
succinctly write down the current condition of your life
and of your business. This can be a bit sobering, but it is
essential for moving forward. It identifies the "positives
and negatives" of your current condition/situation. The
positives may require modification or "tweaking," and
the negatives, of course, will require a definite action
plan.

ACTION PLAN OR CAMPAIGN
TO BECOME UNSTUCK

As the above steps have been completed, you will find
a sense of "relief," clarity, and even enthusiasm, because
you are now gaining back control. You are again at the
rudder of your ship. This is where it becomes "fun!" It
isn't all "clear sailing" but now you are guiding the ship.
   Related to the personal aspect of becoming "unstuck,"
examine each of the vision of success areas and write
down what action you wish to take to achieve your vision
of success. Yes, you may consider this "goal setting,"
therefore you will want to make them "SMART"—
Specific, Measurable, Attainable, Relevant, and Timely.

Related to your business, the process is similar with one big difference. You want to first determine "how the business got where it currently is." One key to business success is to use common sense. That means we learn from our experiences (mistakes or not). So with each of the major business areas, write down how the current condition came to be. It may as simple as "I never paid any attention to it," or "we tried this and that."

The next step is to proceed as above with writing down an action plan for each of the key business areas. Once this has been formulated, it is now just moving forward with the action. CAUTION: this requires discipline, commitment, perseverance, and measurement. This should be the "fun step" of the whole process, because you are now in control. You know your direction, and you are UNSTUCK!!

CHAPTER NINE

*The best and most beautiful things in the world
cannot be seen or even touched—
they must be felt with the heart.*

Beyond the Five Habits of Highly Successful Business People
Some Thoughts and Observations

Forty years plus of being actively involved in business enterprise, has been quite an adventure. During this time, I have always tried to be a "diligent student" of business, and for that matter, life. Not from an academic, philosophical, theoretical perspective, but from a "nuts and bolts" perspective. In this chapter, I share some of my observations and thoughts which, I hope might be helpful to business people (owners and non-owners) as they pursue their "adventures."

BUSINESS 101:
LESSONS IN LIFE FROM BUSINESS

Through the years in business, I have learned valuable lessons which can be directly applied to life. These lessons came directly from my business experiences. Here are some of them.

ATTITUDE

Being in business has taught me the importance of attitude. Not only to have a positive mental attitude, but the role that the correct attitude plays in our success. Attitude is an invaluable guide to instantly improving the way you feel about life, and your place in the world. The correct attitude helps you to effectively deal with adverse situations as well as those that are positive. It is the lubricant for your "psychic engine" that keeps it running smoothly. Sometimes we require an "attitude adjustment," which is normal. This can be done in many ways including attending appropriate seminars, workshops, profound reading, and associating with the right people. Indeed, I believe we draw "psychic energy" from those whom we associate, therefore choose your friends and associates carefully. Avoid those who will drain your "psychic energy." No matter what situation presents itself, if you have the correct attitude, you will make the correct decisions, and every experience will be a growth experience.

PERCEPTION

Our reality is actually based on how and what we perceive. One of the blessings of being in business is that it exposes a person to many situations, circumstances and opportunities. These all influence our perception of reality. If our attitude is correct, our perceptions can lead us to new growth opportunities. These growth opportunities expand our horizons, and will significantly influence our personal lives. In essence, being in business broadens our world of experiences which influences our perceptions of things. This, intern, influences and expands our perceptions of reality in our personal lives.

HEALTH

Being in business has taught me the value of having good health. Without good health, one has a significant handicap in life and business. I learned to respect and value good health, and to not take it for granted. I learned that one has to take time, virtually every day, to maintain good health. Good physical health will enhance good mental health which is essential in being successful in business and life. Sometimes, if we have not been practicing a healthy life style, it is necessary to make the attainment of good health a priority in our life. The "re-attainment" of good health takes time, but is well worth the commitment. Good health is essential to the maintenance of the correct attitude. They are directly related. Keep the correct attitude as you "re-attain" good health, then the good health will sustain your correct attitude. The experiences of business and life are a constant "draw" on our mental and "psychic" energy. With good health, we continually have the reserves to provide the energy that is required.

RESPONSIBILITY

I learned to be responsible for my actions, to not make excuses, and accept the consequences of my decisions. It is tempting to place responsibility for consequences on someone or something else. To do this, actually robs us of the ability to grow and develop. Failures or setbacks have been the chief learning situations for me. Taking responsibility for them allowed me to learn the lesson well, and grow from it.

QUALITY RELATIONSHIPS

I learned the value of developing quality relationships. It takes time and the expenditure of energy to develop quality relationships. Once developed, they need to be nurtured and maintained. Quality relationships are the cornerstones of any real rewarding life. No one is a "rock or an island," and life is full and meaningful when we share it with others who we truly value and who value us.

ECONOMICS

Economics is a very powerful force. Countries have gone to war over economic issues. I learned the power of economics, and to respect basic economic principles. If we violate the basic principles of economics in our life, we are destined to have perpetual turmoil. This turmoil will manifest itself in a variety of ways such as divorce, bankruptcy, and even suicide. All of these terrible life consequences can be avoided by learning and applying the basic laws of economics in our personal lives.

HUMILITY

Over time, business will make one humble, it did me. I began my business career by thinking I was "invincible," and could not fail. I thought that all success was related to my great expertise, talents and wisdom. Business taught me that I was not the center of all things, and that sometimes forces beyond my control will affect my destiny. It taught me that failure is not fatal, but is for learning. I learned the real virtue in life is to make significant contributions to the lives of others, and this can only be done by being humbly in the service of others. I believe that when you are in the service of others, you are actually about the work of your creator.

ACCOUNTABILITY

I learned to be accountable for what I do and say. When we are accountable for our actions, we gain certain strength. This strength provides the power to effectively deal with the issues of life. Being accountable allows us to develop self-respect, and the respect of others who interface with us. This respect, like a magnet, draws people to us, which provides additional opportunities for personal growth and development.

HONESTY

Often in business there is the temptation to sometimes be less than "completely" honest to expedite a situation or our agenda. This may not mean being overtly dishonest, but just not completely honest in our dealing with others. I learned that ultimately, one has to live with themselves and their actions, and knowing that one has dealt with everyone in every situation honestly is a great comfort, and a true builder of character.

FINANCIAL RESPONSIBILITY

If one is to stay in business, one has to operate their business in a fiscally responsible manner. This is also true in our personal life. The true lesson is to live within "our means." The "having" of things just for the sake of having them, or because others have them, is foolish. It is much more valuable to have sound financial security than to "have things." Someone else will always have more, bigger, or better "things." Having the "inner peace of mind" that sound financial responsibility brings is invaluable.

It is obvious that all of these "lessons" in business are interrelated. Not one of them is mutually exclusive, but they all are applicable to our personal life. Taken together, if learned well, and practiced, they will lead to the ultimate goal in our life, which I believe is Joy and Fulfillment.

CORE BELIEFS
OF SUCCESSFUL PEOPLE

I have had a wonderful opportunity to observe successful and unsuccessful people. During these observations, certain "truths" appeared to be consistent as they related to the successful people. I have called these "truths" "Core Beliefs of Successful People."

"WINNERS" ARE NOT BORN, THEY ARE MADE.

There does not seem to be any consistent relationship or correlation between success and education, unique talents, financial resources, or race/ethnicity. It seems to "boil down" to common sense, diligence (I don't like the term "hard work"), knowledge and it application, and perseverance.

THE DOMINANT FORCE IN YOUR EXISTENCE IS THE WAY YOU THINK.

What we think about definitely affects the outcomes of our lives. I do believe that we have both a conscious and subconscious thought process. I remember a comment by Wayne Dyer to the effect that, what is inside of us comes out when we are "squeezed." If we are feeling angry, it comes out. If we are feeling positive it comes out. If we think positive and constructive thoughts, our life will reflect that.

YOU CAN CREATE YOUR OWN REALITY.

We are truly blessed to live in the United States of America! This is still the land of opportunity. If we want something strong enough, and are willing to make the necessary commitments and sacrifices for it, we can create our own reality.

THERE IS SOME BENEFIT TO BE GAINED FROM EVERY ADVERSITY.

As I look back on my modest business career, it seems that virtually all of the valuable lessons that I have learned were the result of "setbacks," "failures" or adversity. I guess, for me, that is my method of learning. I would not say that is true for everyone, but I do know, that adversity really "hammers the lessons home."

EACH ONE OF YOUR BELIEFS IS A CHOICE.

Everything that we do in business, or for the matter in life, is a series of choices. Therefore, it is best that we develop, early on, a strong set of core beliefs and values. They will serve well as the compass to make all of the directional choices in business and life correctly.

YOU ARE NEVER DEFEATED UNTIL YOU ACCEPT DEFEAT AS A REALITY AND QUIT TRYING.

I can remember lying on the football field, face down, wet, mud in my face, knees in excruciating pain, and the person I was supposed to tackle running for a touchdown. Vince Lombardi's words rang in my head, "It is not failure to get knocked down, and it is only failure if you do not get back up." And so it is in business. Learn to accept "no," to have plans altered, and to be disappointed. That is part of the "game." The best part of the game is to stay in it, and keep "playing."

THE ONLY REAL LIMITATIONS ON WHAT YOU CAN ACCOMPLISH ARE THOSE ON YOURSELF.

We can have "abundance" or a "scarcity" mentality. The choice is ours. To me, seeing the world as a place of abundant opportunities has allowed me great freedom, provided great opportunities, and generally has made my life exceedingly joyful. Allow yourself the opportunity to experience life to the fullest, by not setting any limitations on yourself. As President Franklin D. Roosevelt said, "The only thing we have to fear is fear itself."

YOU ALREADY POSSESS THE ABILITY TO EXCEL IN AT LEAST ONE KEY AREA IN YOUR LIFE.

Having good self-confidence is essential to a successful business career. Each of us has "days" when we wonder if we "have what it takes." The good news is that we do, and more importantly, we can get the knowledge that it takes if we come up short in some area. Again, it is perseverance that counts, along with a passion for what we are doing.

THERE CAN BE NO GREAT SUCCESS WITHOUT GREAT COMMITMENT.

One of my favorite quotes is from the German philosopher Goethe: "The moment one definitely commits oneself, then providence moves too. All sorts of things occur to help one that would never otherwise have occurred. A whole stream of events issues from the decision, raising in one's favor all manner of unforeseen incidents and meetings and material assistance which no man could have dreamed would have come his way. Whatever you can do or dream you can, begin it. Boldness has genius, power and magic in it. Begin it now." In my experience, the hard part is first making the commitment. Once done, it is surprising how opportunities start to happen and "things fall into place."

YOU NEED THE SUPPORT AND COOPERATION OF OTHER PEOPLE TO ACHIEVE ANY WORTHWHILE GOAL.

I remember the Paul Simon song who's lyric goes, "I am a rock, I am an island." It is a great song, and if you listen carefully, you realize that no one really is an "island," and we are not alone. We just have to have the proper attitude, and all matter of support and synergy is at our command. Nothing of any great significance can be done without the cooperation of other people. The challenge is to find the key people, engage them, and make sure they receive their reward which is not always financial. Often it is just recognition.

MAKE IT HAPPEN.

Incorporate these core beliefs in your life, and you can be assured of being successful, no matter what your definition of success is and what your endeavors are. Enjoy the journey, the fruits of which will bring you success, happiness and joy.

THE STAGES OF BUSINESS GROWTH

Let's compare the stages of a business's life to that of our own (infancy to "continuity"). I believe there are some valuable lessons to be learned.

Infant to Early Childhood Stage

This is a glorious time. It is an idea ready to birth, or an acquisition about to happen. You actually don't know what you don't know. But it is exciting, stimulating and challenging. Just as you begin to think about what your infant child will turn out to be, you have the same thought for your business. This is a time for plans, "business plans," and action.

From Early Childhood to Early Adolescence Stage

The "newness" of the business has worn off. Now it is the reality of making it work. You learn that the business plan was not "gospel," and many adjustments have to be made along the way. You begin to realize what the "total impact" of being in business means to your life style.

Adolescence ("teenager") Stage

By now, things are going pretty good. You are feeling pretty good about your accomplishments. Although the business plan hasn't been looked at in a while, you are sure with all of the modifications you made to it are the reason you are where you are now. You have "all of the answers."

Adulthood Stage

You are now ready to move from being "the producer" and begin to think in terms of delegation. A whole new world opens up to you with the concurrent challenges. Gosh, you realize that you don't have all of the answers.

Maturity Stage

You now know the meaning of the phrase: "Good decisions come mostly from experience, and most valuable experience comes from making bad decisions." Nevertheless, you now have mastered the art of delegation. The business now has in place processes and systems that carry the business along on a day to day basis. The business is no longer dependent on you for day to day operations and success. You are off of the treadmill.

"Continuement" Stage

Now, the business owner begins to think of "retirement." In reality, there is not such a thing in store for him or her. A better term might be "continument." Retirement is that nirvana place where life is worry free. It is an illusion of contentment. Unfortunately, it is, indeed, an illusion. The business owner and hopefully, the business will continue, i.e., "Continuement." This can take the form of the business being sold to a third party, employees, or family members. In which case, the business owner is now looking for something else to keep their brain cells from decaying. Or, maybe the business is now run by trusted employees/part owners, and the business owner becomes a mentor, and/or a visionary looking for new paths/directions for the business. In the case of a departing business owner, the cycle begins again for the new owner (albeit, at accelerated early stages, and the "Continuement" business owner returns to the early cycles of a new adventure.

POST SCRIPT

In keeping with our life cycle analogy, what about death? In the case of business, this, unlike life, can be avoided. In life, it is just the next level of progression. However, in business it is a tragedy! The business owner either did not recognize the stages of business growth/ maturity, or ignored them. One of the great blessings of small to medium size businesses, is that if it is a "well run," positive cash flowing, and mature business, there will always be someone wanting to own it. That is the "golden parachute" opportunity of business ownership.

A LITTLE BUSINESS PARABLE
ABOUT INTEGRITY

A successful businessman was growing old and knew it was time to choose a successor to take over the business.

Instead of choosing one of his Directors or his children, he decided to do something different. He called all the young executives in his company together.

He said, "It is time for me to step down and choose the next CEO. I have decided to choose one of you." The young executives were shocked, but the boss continued. "I am going to give each one of you a SEED today—one very special SEED. I want you to plant the seed, water it, and come back here one year from today with what you have grown from the seed I have given you. I will then judge the plants that you bring, and the one I choose will be the next CEO."

One man, named Jim, was there that day and he, like the others, received a seed. He went home and excitely, told his wife the story. She helped him get a pot, soil and compost and he planted the seed. Every day, he would water it and watch to see if it had grown.

After about three weeks, some of the other executives began to talk about their seeds and the plants that were beginning to grow.

Jim kept checking his seed, but nothing ever grew. Three weeks, four weeks, five weeks went by, still nothing.

By now, others were talking about their plants, but Jim didn't have a plant and he felt like a failure.

Six months went by -- still nothing in Jim's pot. He just knew he had killed his seed. Everyone else had trees and tall plants, but he had nothing Jim didn't say anything to his colleagues, however, he just kept watering and fertilizing the soil, he so wanted the seed to grow.

A year finally went by and all the young executives of the company brought their plants to the CEO for inspection.

Jim told his wife that he wasn't going to take an empty pot. But she asked him to be honest about what happened. Jim felt sick to his stomach, it was going to be the most embarrassing moment of his life, but he knew his wife was right. He took his empty pot to the boardroom.

When Jim arrived, he was amazed at the variety of plants grown by the other executives. They were beautiful - in all shapes and sizes. Jim put his empty pot on the floor and many of his colleagues laughed, a few felt sorry for him!

When the CEO arrived, he surveyed the room and greeted his young executives.

Jim just tried to hide in the back. "My, what great plants, trees and flowers you have grown," said the CEO. "Today one of you will be appointed the next CEO!"

All of a sudden, the CEO spotted Jim at the back of the room with his empty pot. He ordered the Financial Director to bring him to the front. Jim was terrified. He thought, "The CEO knows I'm a failure! Maybe he will have me fired!"

When Jim got to the front, the CEO asked him what had happened to his seed, Jim told him the whole story.

The CEO asked everyone to sit down except Jim. He looked at Jim, and then announced to the young executives, "Behold your new Chief Executive Officer! His name is Jim!"

Jim couldn't believe it. Jim couldn't even grow his seed.

"How could he be the new CEO?" the others asked.

Then the CEO said, "One year ago today, I gave everyone in this room a seed. I told you to take the seed, plant it, water it, and bring it back to me today. But I gave you all boiled seeds; they were dead, it was not possible for them to grow. All of you, except Jim, have brought me trees and plants and flowers. When you found that the seed would not grow, you substituted another seed for the one I gave you. Jim was the only one with the courage and honesty to bring me a pot with my seed in it. Therefore, he is the one who will be the new Chief Executive Officer!"

REMEMBER:

- If you plant honesty, you will reap trust
- If you plant goodness, you will reap friends
- If you plant humility, you will reap greatness
- If you plant perseverance, you will reap contentment
- If you plant consideration, you will reap perspective
- If you plant hard work, you will reap success
- If you plant forgiveness, you will reap reconciliation

So, be careful what you plant now; it will determine what you will reap later. Think about it.

HOW TO EFFECTIVELY HANDLE STRESS

It is an acknowledged fact that stress can be a "killer." It creates chemical reactions in your body that, if they become "chronic," can be very detrimental to your health and welfare. Managing it is just as important as managing your business. Here are 12 ways to help you manage stress.

1. Spend time reflecting on your life – look at the big picture. (When stressed, we tend to develop tunnel vision.)
2. Exercise regularly – it relieves tension. Asking a friend to exercise with you will provide accountability and make it more fun.
3. Talk difficult issues over with a trusted friend or trusted advisors.
4. Journal – write down all your concerns and how you feel about them, then throw the paper away and let it go.
5. Take time out to meditate, pray or go for a walk and observe nature – the trees and flowers, listen to the birds, and watch the ever-changing cloud formations. Spend time with people, get to know them and develop deeper relationships. In other words, break up your routine.
6. Get adequate sleep and rest at night.
7. Plan time for fun – laughter is good medicine, indeed, it is the lubricant of life. Taking time

out to relax and play shouldn't be considered a luxury.

8. If you face a stressful situation that is beyond your control, put it in perspective by asking yourself how it will feel and what impact it will have on you five years. Focus on providing unrequited service to another, it will remove you from your stressful situation.

9. Focus on what is positive in your life and business, and see the glass as half full. Turn your attention to things that have gone well.

10. View stressful situations, large and small, as opportunities to learn. Stop, step back and think about ways you could benefit from them. Post-It® notes were invented as solutions to frustrating problems.

11. Take five-minute vacations. Stop work for five minutes, relax, breathe deeply and think about something fun and pleasant. This can refresh your mind and you'll return to the project with new clarity.

12. When you've completed a stressful task, reward yourself with something you enjoy. For me, it's a hot fudge sundae!

Some thoughts on
WEALTH ACCUMULATION AND
MAINTENANCE

"Wealth is the ability to truly (fully) experience life"
—Henry David Thoreau

Early in my Dental career a mature gentleman came in for his Hygiene appointment. At the conclusion of his appointment I visited with him. He indicated that he was impressed with my "work ethic" and would share a secret to "wealth." I pulled my stool up close to the dental chair to listen to his "secret." He said, "You will work hard to gain your degree of wealth, but you will have to work twice as hard to keep it." At the time, I didn't think much of that advice. In subsequent years, I have come to realize how very profound his statement ("secret") was.

Accumulation of Wealth
- Inherit it, or win the lottery: then, see maintenance below.
- Start early or NOW to form the habit of saving.
- Live below your means.
- Avoid debt with the exception of home, vehicle and business (have a definite   plan in place to retire the business debt).
- Avoid quick, "get rich" temptations. The true road is one of consistent, diligent, patient, small steps.
- Have balance with your assets:

Real Estate, Equities, Commodities, Annuities, Precious Metals, Etc.
- Strive to have multiple streams of consistent income.
- If in business, make payment to yourself a priority.
- If in business have an exit strategy.
- Have a trusted, competent financial advisor.
- The government will not provide for you.
- True "Wealth" is not "Things," it is Quality Relationships;
  - Family, Friends, Associates, Colleagues, and Spirituality.
  - It is having a purpose to your life, and being comfortable with yourself and how you treat others.
  - It is unrequited service to others.

Maintenance of Wealth

- You will work diligently (hard) to acquire some degree of wealth. You will have to work twice as hard (diligently) to maintain it.
- The habits you form early in life, or NOW change to, have or will determine the probability of your success in accumulating and maintaining wealth.
- Mistakes are OK, they are for learning. Do not make the same one twice.
- As you are young, prudent risks are OK, but as you age, be conservative, because there is

less time for you to "recover" from losses or missteps.

- If you have not had a competent, trusted financial advisor up to this time, it is now very appropriate to have one.

TEN AXIOMS FOR BUSINESS SUCCESS

Axioms are self-evident or universally recognized truths. They are things we probably know, but often do not routinely practice. It has been my experience that understanding and practicing certain axioms lead to success, be it in business or life. Here are the axioms I use and practice.

1. Treat every person as you would want to be treated if your roles were reversed. Yes, I know, it is the Golden Rule, but it is paramount to practice for sustainable success.
2. True joy, be it in business or life, comes from providing unrequited service to others.
3. Hire for strength of character and attitude, then train for skills and techniques.
4. Profit (or loss) is only the score card of how well you are playing the game.
5. Playing the game is what is important.
6. Effective communication is the main thread in the fiber of business success, and for that matter, establishing and maintaining quality relationships.
7. For effective communication, first understand the other person, then seek to have them understand you.
8. Failures and setbacks are not fatal. They are to

learn from; they are absolutely necessary for building character.

9. Always give more service and value than is expected or required.

10. The true values are joy, happiness, and peace of mind (comfortable in your "own skin"). All else is subordinate to them.

EPILOG

*Cherish your visions and your dreams as they
are the children of your soul, the blueprints
of your ultimate achievements.*

THE FOUR SEASONS
OF A BUSINESS

All living things have a life cycle, and so it is with a business entity. Just as in nature in which there are four seasons (Spring, Summer, Fall and Winter), there are four seasons to a business.

*"Listen, can you hear it? Spring's sweet cantata.
The strains of grass pushing through the snow.
The song of buds swelling on the vine.
The tender timpani of a baby robin's heart. Spring."*
—Diane Frolov and Andrew Schneider

Spring is the season of "birth." Birth in business may be the startup of a new business or the acquisition of an existing business. In either case, it is the beginning of a new experience (adventure) for the business owner. It entails the development of business plans, marketing plans, acquisition of capital, establishing of new relationships (with vendors, customers, employees, an professionals such as attorneys, accountants, bankers, and insurance representatives), checking out competition, determining the business's niche in the market, to name just a few. It is an exhilarating and exciting time. It is a time of discovery.

"Summer afternoon - Summer afternoon...
the two most beautiful words in the English language."
—Henry James

As the Summer season arrives, the business owner starts to mature into the "running" of the business. The relationship building process continues with some relationships being nurtured and groomed, and some being discarded. This is the time when systems are being developed, implemented and refined. Finance continues to be an important factor with focus on developing adequate positive cash flow and profitability. It is a time of planting the seeds which will bring the fruits of business success in the seasons to come. The exhilaration and excitement of "being in business" as business continues. Every day is a new adventure which brings new challenges and ads to the log of experience of the business owner.

"There is a harmony
In autumn, and a lustre in its sky,
Which through the summer is not heard or seen,
As if it could not be, as if it had not been!"
—Percy Bysshe Shelley

By the Fall season, the business and business owner are now matured. The systems put in place during the summer season have been refined and are operating smoothly. The relationships built during the Spring and Summer are now well developed and are ones of high quality. The business is well entrenched in its market niche. Profitability and positive cash flow are well established. This is the season of enjoyment of the fruits of what has been planted in the previous seasons. It is also the season for reflection, as the wise business owner now realizes that the next season is Winter, and appropriate planning must now take place to accommodate that season.

"O Winter! ruler of the inverted year . . .
I crown thee king of intimate delights,
Fireside enjoyments, home-born happiness,
And all the comforts that the lowly roof Of undisturbed
Retirement, and the hours
of long uninterrupted evening, know."
—William Cowper

As the leaves begin to fall from the trees in the fall season, harkening the arrival of Winter, so it is in the Winter season of the business. The business owner now must prepare for the eventual transition from the business. Although, the business owner still has the "love of the business" (just as love of life), he/she realizes that it is time to pass the torch. The energy present during the Spring and Summer seasons is no longer present. Possibly the focus, creativity and inventiveness of the business owner are not as strong as in previous seasons. The business entity has grown and matured, and requires new energy, new "sowing of seeds." It is a bitter sweet time for the business owner, but nevertheless a time that requires recognition and action.

If the successful business is to live beyond its owner; it is the owner's responsibility to plan for the transition to a new owner. This planning is as important as the initial business plan, and all of the systems that have been developed. A misstep at this point could be disastrous, but careful planning and implementation will ensure the continued success of the business. Just as the proud father "hands over" his daughter at her wedding, so it is that the owner "hands over" the reins of the business to another who will revel in the "cycles" yet to come.

> *"If winter is slumber and spring is birth,*
> *and summer is life,*
> *then autumn rounds out to be reflection.*
> *It's a time of year when the leaves*
> *are down and the harvest is in*
> *and the perennials are gone.*
> *Mother Earth just closed up the drapes*
> *on another year and it's time*
> *to reflect on what's come before."*
> —Mitchell Burgess

The point of this parable is that a business is a vibrant, "living" entity. It, just as all living things, has a cycle of life. The prudent business owner recognizes the "seasons of the business," and plans for them at the outset of entering into business. Proper planning for each season at the beginning will enhance the enjoyment and success of the business owner throughout the life of the business.

Unfortunately, in our society we have not been focused on planning for the future. In living in the United States of America, most of us have been blessed with an abundance of opportunity, wealth, and comforts. We have not been a people who have saved or put away for the future. The attitude seems to be, the future will take care of itself. In business this attitude can be disastrous. If we as business owners do not plan for the future, we can be assured that there will not be a bright future. As prudent business owners, we need to begin with the end in mind, and recognize the milestones of the seasons in our business. If we have, at the start, the completion of the cycle in our mind's eye, the business will be everlasting- the greatest legacy a business owner could hope for. The future will indeed be bright and one that holds rich rewards.

Appendix A

EFFECTIVE DELEGATING MADE EASY

Let's begin with first things first, the "**why delegate**." Of course it may seem self-evident. It is to allow the delegator to leverage their time and talent. Certainly, that is a significant reason. Being able to leverage one's self in terms of time, energy and tasks is vitally important to growing a business. But, there are other reasons, which may be equally as important.

People leadership is critical to the growth and development of a business. The people in the business enterprise are the "heart" of the business. To master the "art and science" of effective delegation means being able to effectively lead people. People require leadership, and things are managed. To be an effective delegator means to grow and invest in the people of your business. Many years ago, my business enterprises, although relative small and new at the time, were growing and thriving. I was "managing" my people well, or so I thought. In actuality, it was all about me, and much less about them. During a staff meeting in which both managers and Dentists were present, one of the Dentists made the comment that "Lee is a legend in his own mind." Of course everyone laughed, as did I. However, that comment stuck with me long after that meeting. I realized that I needed to change my approach to the "management" of my businesses. I began to read all that I could find on leadership. Soon I radically altered my approach to the management of my businesses, and adopted the principles and techniques I had read. Low and behold, the businesses began to really "take off." People were coming up with new and innovative ways for us to advance our businesses. My real job became listening to my people, and incorporating their great ideas and suggestions. In part, I became a "facilitator." This is one of the real reasons, "the why," to master effective delegation. It is really about leadership.

Another vital reason to master the art and science of effective delegation is to create INTRINSIC VALUE in your business. Simply put, if your business is highly dependent upon you and your daily input, it has little value. On the other hand, if your business "runs without" your daily input (being off of the treadmill), your business has great INTRINSIC VALUE. Why, because someone else can "take over" the business without it missing a step. There will always be persons looking for a business with INTRINSIC VALUE.

There are **three keys to effective delegation**: responsibility, authority, and accountability.

> The delegator must give full responsibility to the delegate. There must not be any question as to who has the responsibility for the task or initiative.
>
> Secondly, the delegator must give authority to the delegate. All must know that the delegate has been give full authority to carry out the tasks and responsibilities assigned to them.
>
> Then, there must be methodology in place to measure the performance of the delegate. This is known as accountability.

Next, it must be determined **what to delegate**. Here is a list (not all inclusive) of what to delegate:

- Reoccurring tasks;
- Less important decisions or tasks;
- Time consuming details (although remember sometimes success is "in the details")
- Look at the position description of the delegator. Yes, the delegator should also have a position description, and it can be used to determine some of the items above.
- Using the "SMART" principle can also be helpful to determine what to delegate.
- **S**IMPLE, keep it simple

- **MEASUREABLE**, whatever is delegated must be measureable,
- **ACHIEVEABLE**, whatever is delegated must be realistically achievable,
- **REALISTIC**, that which is delegated must be realistic, and no "pie in the sky" unrealistic objectives,
- **TIME**, set realistic times frames to achieve the objectives.

Just as important as what to delegate is **what NOT to delegate.** There are at least two items that must never be delegated.

> Never delegate praise. This should always be done by the delegator, unless it is within the position description of the delegate as he/she leads those that report to them.
>
> Never delegate discipline. This, too, should always be done by the delegator, again, unless it is within the position description of the delegate as he/she leads those that report to them.

Now, we come to the topic of **"who to delegate to."** This is very important, and if we remember that one of the major responsibilities of the delegator (leader) is to "grow their people," it makes this much easier to do. Do NOT delegate to:

- Your "right hand person." They will only become overworked and others will wonder why they are the "favorite."
- Not the most busy person for the same reasons as above.
- Not the person who "always comes through," for many of the same reasons as above. This is often a crutch used by ineffective delegators.

So, delegate to the person that you want "to grow," and has the correct attitude.

We have already touched on the overarching reason (the why) to delegate. However, here are important reasons from the perspective of the potential delegate:

It is a powerful motivator of people. It provides recognition, advancement, increased responsibility, allows people to make their own missteps which is a learning experience, it provides challenges which can be stimulating, and often it provides valuable feedback to the delegator.

This brings us to the "**how to effectively delegate**." Here are the simple steps to follow:

- Select the person.
- Set clear, attainable objectives.
- Assign the project and/or responsibility.

- TRAIN the person, obtain their input, provide proper background, and support including alternatives and anticipated results. This should be a discussion and the result is clarity.
- Obtain a "meeting of the minds" which should include, degree of authority, resources and options such as:
- "Get it done."
- "Do it, but keep me advised."
- "Do all of the foundation work, and check with me before taking action."
- "I will tell you what, how, and when to do it." (obviously this is NOT effective delegation)
- At this point, decide on follow up, i.e., "who contacts who," and when. This is a critical step. Communication is vitally important. Do not leave this to chance.
- Agree as to how performance is to be measured and when. Again, another vital step in the process. Without measurement (accountability), effective delegation becomes ineffective.

It is important that the delegator maintains control of the process or project.

Here is a "twist." The delegator must remain as much aware of what is "NOT HAPPENING," as what is happening. In other words, stay engaged.

Always be intuitive, in other words, pay attention to your "gut feelings."

Appendix B

RAPID RESULTS SALES PROCESS

(The Simple Sales Program That Really Works)

OVERVIEW

The "Four C's" represents the Rapid Results Sales Process (technique) from the beginning, to the sale, and beyond. It has four stages (steps) which include: The Contacts (C1), the second stage is Connection (C2), the third stage is Credibility (C3), and the fourth stage, Client (C4). Forget "selling prospects." Think in terms of serving others and building quality relationships in an organized, accountable manner. The specific program is easily incorporated into the Outlook CRM software, and can be adapted to other contact management software programs.

STEP ONE: CONTACTS (C1)

The C1 includes business associates, friends, family, leads groups, chambers of commerce, and networking events. It represents all of the people you know. It also will include the contacts from leads groups, meet ups, networking events, etc. Make a list (maybe a database, contact resource management, card scanner, etc.) of all the above including names, telephone numbers, email addresses and possibly company affiliation. Keep it SIMPLE. Organize your list into people easiest to contact, first. Then the next easiest and so on, until you come to the ones that you know will take mental discipline to contact. But, put them on the list also. I know this sounds like the beginning of a MLM venture, it's not so stay with me. EVENTUALLY, YOU WILL NEVER HAVE TO GO BACK TO THIS STEP!!

STEP TWO: CONNECTIONS (C2)

This represents the organized list of people to contact, to have a conversation with, your CONNECTIONS. You begin by contacting (telephone preferred or email) those on your list that you consider the easiest for you to make contact with and have a conversation. Your contact is NOT a sales call. It is a call to establish an opportunity to get together for you to learn how you may be able to SERVE them, and possibly create a MUTUALLY BENEFICIAL business relationship.

STEP THREE: CREDIBILITY (C3)

At this stage you have a face to face "visit" with the contact. This represents the transfer of your contacts/connections to one of an ongoing business relationship. Ideally, they will become "raving fans" or at least "advocates" of you and your product/ service. At the very minimal, they are comfortable in referring to you. You now know how to serve them, they know how to serve you, and may even become a contact which moves into the next step, A CLIENT (C4).

STEP FOUR: CLIENT (C4)
Plus Boosters and Allies

This is the step, and the previous one, are where the "buying" takes place. Buying in 2 respects: buying your goods or services (Client), and "buying you" (Credible Connection). Here you gain a commitment for them to buy your product/service and/or buy into you, i.e. comfortable referring you to their sphere of influence. This is not "closing the sale." I don't like the term, "close the sale." Nothing has been "closed," indeed you have just "opened a door." You now provide your product/service to exceed their expectation, and the expectations of the ones they refer to you The objective is to convert them into a "Boosters," or "Allies," and continue them in the Four C's process.

BOOSTERS AND ALLIES
(An Integral Part of the Rapid Results Sales Process)

- Boosters are usually clients or former clients who have been favorably impressed with you, your product/service.
- Boosters may be persons from C3, Credibility, that really like you, but have not been clients. This is, however unusual.
- Allies are people you have impressed in your credibility visits, but are not usually clients (initially). If a person is a client/ally, you have done something wrong. (They should have become Boosters)
- You are "top of the mind" for a booster, and they want to share the "good stuff" with their sphere of influence people.
- Allies like you, and "buy into" you and/or your product or service.
- You are just not "top of the mind" for them, and they will not put their "neck on the line" for you.
- Each requires a different follow up- follow through process.
- You want to design your follow up program so that you "touch" the Allies more often than the Boosters. Possibly touch the Boosters quarterly and the Allies monthly.
- The manner in which you "touch each" will be different. Sending a brief, but valuable email to the Allies monthly through the Outlook Business

Contact Manager/ Rapid Results Sales Process program is suggested. Doing a "SendOutCard" or other such program/gift is appropriate for Boosters.
- The important thing is that you do, and consistently "touch" them.

HOW TO DO IT: YOUR GAMEPLAN
(The Great Game of Business & Life)

- Make your list/database.
- Organize your list to be a functional contact management system. Keep it simple. At the "top," have the easiest contacts to make down to the "hardest."
- It is now a process like a funnel: commit to making a certain number of calls or emails (connections) per time period (day, week, etc.). Be realistic. The object is to set appointments to fill the stage C2. Once there are prospects in the C2 stage, focus on moving selected ones to stage C3, Credibility. This is an ongoing process, which requires discipline. "Rome was not built in a day." You are building a QUALITY referral program, that in time you will not have to repeat steps one and two. You will have a CONTINUING FLOW OF NEW OPPORTUNITIES. From Stage C3 (Credibility) focus on moving these people into Stage C4 (Client). Remember, they may not buy from you now that is ok. If they do, great. If they don't, determine if they buy "into you, your product or service." If they do,

they belong in stage C3, and also put into the Allies "touching" process. If they don't, move them back to stage C2 or C1. Never delete them from your database. It is surprising how many eventually come back to C3 or C4. That is because you didn't try to sell them, but tried to serve them.

ACCOUNTABILITY, ACCOUNTABILITY, ACCOUNTABILITY

No process or system is complete without this vital step. For many, it is the hardest one. It is ABSOLUTELY ESSENTIAL to the success of your sales program. Make a commitment (to yourself, or your coach) as to the following:

- Complete your lists, Business Contact Management, etc.) This is Contacts, C1. Give it a date for completion.
- Commit to the # of calls/conversations into your Contacts per time frame and notate it each time it is completed. Be realistic. Remember it is like a funnel. You start with a realistically large number to get to the final smaller number. This is stage C2, Connections. The objective is to have people commit to a face to face visit, Stage C3 Credibility.
- Commit to the # of appointments (credibility visits) to build your stage C3, Credibility per time frame and notate it each time it is completed.
- Identify the # of Clients (C4) you converted from

Stage C3. Also notate those that become Boosters or at least Allies.

- An important part of this process is to create a continuing, "touching," process for the Boosters and Allies as explained above.
- If you are having trouble implementing or following your game plan:
- Ask yourself if you truly believe in the process/game plan.
- Ask yourself if you truly believe in you and your product/service.
- Reduce your numbers to a smaller # until such time as you are more comfortable with the process.
- Obtain help and encouragement for a trusted friend, associate or business advisor.

The Rapid Results Process (program) generates reports that track the appropriate numbers on a weekly, monthly, quarterly and annual basis. These reports allow the user to adjust their process to fit the results they are seeking.

PRINCIPLES TO REMEMBER

- PERSEVERANCE is one important key to business success.
- TIME: One of your most important assets; use it wisely and efficiently

- You must have patience, discipline and personal ACCOUNTABILITY.
- Understand where you are in the process and don't try to go immediately from step one to step four. There may be exceptions, but they are rare and not the norm.
- Portions of the process can be DELEGATED!
- There is no END POINT. It is a continuing process and adventure. Success is not an endpoint/destination, but a path traveled. So enjoy the trip.

Appendix C1

RELATIONSHIP CHECKUP

OVERVIEW

The periodic performance review, "employee review," has been the norm for evaluating employee performance. It does not promote teamwork, constructive two - way (employee to supervisor and visa versa) communication, nor does it contribute to long term positive employee relationships. The performance review is appropriate for a new employee during their initial 30 to 90 days of employment. This period of employment should not be considered a "probation period". It should be termed an "orientation period' for the new employee. They expect input from management during their initial employment, and it is appropriate for management to give constructive evaluation of the new employee's performance at this time. After the initial employment period the relationship checkup is more effective than a performance evaluation in accomplishing what most companies' desire: a motivated, productive, long-term employee, and a business culture of harmony and productivity.

Every position in an organization is important or it should not exist. The relationship checkup acknowledges this principle. There is no "hierarchy" in modern, effective organizations. The relationship checkup stresses effective teamwork rather than "superior-subordinate" positioning. The staff member is given the opportunity at least twice a year to dialogue with their team leader (supervisor) about virtually everything regarding their employment, including constructive critique of management. This approach to staff leadership produces superior results in business culture development and employee performance.

PROTOCOL

A new employee should be given the relationship checkup form during their initial orientation to initially acquaint them with the concept. The concepts and principles should be explained to them at that time. They should be made aware that they will have a "traditional" employee evaluation during their initial (30 - 90 days) of employment, and the format of that evaluation should be given during their orientation. They are advised that after that, at their six months' anniversary of employment, the relationship checkup will be performed. It is appropriate to conduct a relationship checkup twice a year from that time forward.

At the appropriate time, the employee is given a relationship checkup form and an "appointment" is set. Usually an hour is more than enough time to conduct the relationship checkup. The employee is instructed as to how to complete the form, and advised that their supervisor will also complete one side of the form (side A).

The supervisor and employee independently complete the appropriate sides of the form detailing the employee's "strong areas," "growth areas" (not deficient areas), "goals to be accomplished," and "comments" sections. These independent responses are compared. If they are not congruent, dialogue is initiated to clarify each person's position, and bring them into harmony. It is imperative that the supervisor and employee are congruent in how they see the employee's strengths, and growth areas, and goals.

In the "goals to be accomplished" section, it is important that both supervisor and employee mutually agree on the goals to be accomplished before the next relationship checkup. It is also important that the goals are specific, measurable, and time frames established. If they cannot be measured in terms of attainment they are useless. This section is usually modified at the time of the relationship checkup visit, and it is important that both the supervisor and the employee have the goals written down. It is easiest to write them on the employee's form which is copied and the original kept in the employee's personnel folder, with the copy given to the employee.

After the comments section has been reviewed, the form is turned over, and the employee is encouraged to discuss the 20 areas that they have checked in the vertical columns.

It is very important for the supervisor to <u>take notes</u> during this discussion, and to <u>not become defensive</u>. This is an opportunity for the supervisor to gather significant information. This is a time for exploring the employee's true feelings about their, job, the organization, and if handled properly, will give the supervisor the opportunity to enhance the relationship with the employee. It is not necessary, at this time, for the supervisor to give conclusive responses, "give excuses," or be argumentative. The supervisor should repeat what the employee has said to be sure that there is a clear understanding of the points the employee has made. At the conclusion of the review of the 20 statements, the supervisor should schedule a definite follow up appointment to readdress those points that require additional discussion, although this may not be required. This will allow the supervisor time to reflect on what has been said, and determine the best response which will enhance the relationship with the employee. It is very important that the date for the follow up meeting be kept. This will demonstrate to the employee that they are important, and that the supervisor is sincere.

The follow up meeting is conducted in a manner so as to have open, candid, and sincere discussion of the topics of concern for the employee. At its conclusion both parties must feel that there has been constructive, positive resolution to areas of concern. In the areas of compensation adjustment or position advancement, changes can be tied to definite performance goals. Compensation enhancement or changes should not be tied to the relationship checkup interview. Changes should be initiated at a date after the relationship checkup appointment. This will prevent the syndrome of the employee expecting compensation adjustment at the time of the relationship checkup, which is usually the case with performance reviews. It must be stressed to the employee that there is significant value in having a relationship checkup other than a "potential raise," and to differentiate this activity from an "employee review."

The challenge for management is not in conducting the relationship checkups, but actually doing them for each employee on a timely basis (usually twice a year). If management is diligent in doing the relationship checkups for each employee on a timely manner, the results are very positive in terms of staff harmony, motivation, positive culture enhancement, and productivity.

Appendix C2

XYZ COMPANY

RELATIONSHIP CHECK-UP

DATE OF INTERVIEW_____

EMPLOYEE_____

EMPLOYEE SIGNATURE_____

STRONG AREAS_____

GROWTH AREAS_____

GOALS TO BE ACCOMPLISHED BEFORE NEXT
INTERVIEW_____

SUPERVISOR/EMPLOYEE COMMENTS

_____

NEXT INTERVIEW DATE_____

INTERVIEWER/EVALUATOR SIGNATURE_____

RELATIONSHIP CHECK-UP MANAGEMENT EVALUATION	STRONGLY AGREE	AGREE	DON'T KNOW	DISAGREE	STRONGLY DISAGREE
1. OUR STAFF IS WELL ORGANIZED.					
2. MY DUTIES ARE CLEARLY DEFINED.					
3. MY WORKLOAD IS JUST ABOUT RIGHT.					
4. THE MANAGER LETS ME KNOW WHAT IS EXPECTED OF ME.					
5. MY CO-WORKERS ARE VERY FRIENDLY.					
6. MY CO-WORKERS DO THEIR JOBS WELL.					
7. I FEEL FREE TO DISCUSS PROBLEMS OR COMPLAINTS WITH MY SUPERVISOR.					
8. I AM WELL INFORMED OF CHANGES IN THE OFFICE THAT WILL					
9. I HAVE ADEQUATE SUPPLIES AND EQUIPMENT TO DO MY JOB.					
10. I AM PAID FAIRLY IN RELATION TO MY RESPONSIBILITIES.					
11. MANAGEMENT ASKS FOR/USES OUR IDEAS.					
12. PERSONNEL POLICIES ARE STATED CLEARLY.					
13. I AM SATISFIED WITH OUR FRINGE BENEFITS.					
14. STAFF MEMBERS ARE WILLING TO HELP EACH OTHER.					
15. I HAVE THE AUTHORITY I NEED TO PERFORM MY JOB WELL.					
16. MY WORKING HOURS ARE SATISFACTORY.					
17. I AM SATISFIED WITH THE NUMBER OF PAID HOLIDAYS AND					
18. I AM SATISFIED WITH MY POTENTIAL FOR ADVANCEMENT WITHIN THE ORGANIZATION.					
19. I LIKE MY JOB THE WAY IT IS.					
20. I KNOW WHERE I STAND WITH MANAGEMENT.					

ABOUT THE AUTHOR

Lee Thomas grew up on the central coast of California. The little town he grew up in, San Luis Obispo, did not have home delivery of the daily newspaper so, when he was in the fourth grade in elementary school, he would sell newspapers on the corner in front of the drugstore. After several months, he noticed that there were no other kids selling newspapers on the corners, so he persuaded several of his friends to have their own corner newspaper "stands." After school, he would get the papers from the publisher, The Telegram Tribune, and deliver some to each corner, and return to "his corner" to sell the balance. At the end of each day, his buddies would bring their remaining papers to him, and they would "divvy" up the proceeds, with Lee taking one cent for his "management of the enterprise." He would then return the unsold papers to the publisher and "settle up" each day. This happened five days a week. Later during the summer he "partnered" with another friend, and they would go to Morro Bay, on the coast, and clean the fish that the persons had caught during the day on their fishing excursions. This paid BIG money as they each received twenty cents for each gunny sack of fish that they cleaned. In a day's work, they could each clean 10 to 15 or more sacks of fish.

So, it would seem that the "entrepreneurial" gene was actually in him since birth.

It wasn't always good though. When he took a job out of college as a Sales Engineer for a small company in San Jose, California, and he was their first Sales Engineer. Things went really well, or so he thought. After about 22 months, the company had more than doubled their revenues. He had become the Sales Manager, with responsibility over three other sales people. Although his compensation had grown modestly, he had his thoughts set on becoming an equity partner in the business. His boss, a Mr. McDaniel, was the main owner, and a person with an acknowledged temper. He had a minority partner, Henry Griffoul who was in charge of the production. Lee passed his idea past Henry, who thought it was reasonable, but cautioned, "remember "Mack" has a temper, so be careful." One Saturday morning Lee approached "Mack" and made his proposal, explaining how very well the company had done because of HIS (Lee's) efforts, and asked for a 10% interest in the company. Mr. McDaniel looked at Lee, then up at the ceiling, then back at Lee. His response was, "Clean out your desk, and put your keys on my desk, you are through. I will take you home!"

A big lesson learned: When you work for someone else, your career destiny is in their hands.

After another Sales Engineering job with a national firm in which Lee happened to be in the right place at the right time, and made a substantial income, he was offered a significant advancement. It meant relocation to Des Plaines, Illinois. Living in Illinois was not too appealing. It was now time to re-kindle the old entrepreneurial coals. Lee submitted his resignation, made the decision to attempt to enter Dental School, which was a big leap of faith since his undergraduate GPA was only 2.1 on a 4 point scale. Nevertheless, after taking appropriate pre-Dental college courses while working evenings in the machine shop at Hewlett Packard in Palo Alto, California, he was accepted at the School of Dental Medicine at the University of Pittsburgh, Pittsburgh, Pennsylvania.

In 1973, after graduating and completing an internship in Anesthesia, Lee and his wife came to Denver, Colorado, and the "adventures began."

Along the way he has owned, managed, and sold 15 businesses in 10 different industries with annual revenues ranging from under $50,000 to over $8,000,000. These businesses included 16 Dental offices, 23 Childcare centers, a Plumbing/Heating Company, an Automobile Dealership/Modifier, and 12 others.

Currently, through Integrity Business Solutions, a dba of Integrity Business Ventures, LLC, Lee and his associates help people who want to go into business, people in business who may be "stuck" or facing challenges, and people who want to exit their business successfully and "in style."

This book is a compilation of the practical lessons and wisdom that Lee has learned and gained as a serial entrepreneur. It is intended to be a practical guide to help other entrepreneurs reach their visions of success, and enjoy the journey along the way.

The services offered by Integrity Business Solutions provide business owners the following <u>outcomes</u>:

With more than 40+years in business, we view business as a Great Game. Albeit, a very serious game, it has "players," strategies, rules/boundaries, basic principles, techniques, and "measurement." Attracting the right players, having the right "game plan," making the right game decisions, overcoming the competition, and enjoying the rewards of success are all a part of the Great Game of Business. To have a skilled coach/"business partner" to guide you along the way is of great value.

In today's Great Game of Business, having a well-qualified, competent Business Coach/Advisor/ Mentor gives, you, the business owner, the competitive edge required to succeed.

A skilled and experienced Business Coach/Advisor/ Mentor can take the business owner's business from the "average performance level" to the "excellence performance level." From "having a job" to one of the "joys of your life."

A favorite business axioms is: "Most good decisions come from experience, and most valuable experience comes from making bad decisions"

We have been "in the trenches," "made the bad and good decisions," and now share that experience and wisdom with our clients for their Success.

FINANCIAL

- Put more money in your bank: Increase your cash flow almost immediately.
- Determine the "Key Performance Indicators"(critical numbers) to manage your business' performance.
- Master financial statement analysis for effective business financial management.
- Do cash flow projections to eliminate "cash crunches."

MARKETING AND SALES

- Utilize marketing techniques that are proven and work!
- Develop and implement a cost effective marketing strategy.
- Identify market niche(s) and how to exploit them.
- Gain access to competition and strategies to compete effectively.
- Identify additional target markets and how to penetrate them.

- Increase sales with our unique "Rapid Results Sales" program.
- Learn effective database management techniques to increase sales.

PERSONNEL MANAGEMENT

- Create an effective team with our proven techniques.
- Create effective position descriptions and accountabilities.
- Learn effective interviewing techniques (get the right person the first time).
- Learn practical techniques for training, motivating, and terminating employees.
- Develop effective communications modalities.
- Learn quality relationship building techniques to maintain employees and customers.

WORK ON, NOT IN, YOUR BUSINESS (Business Operations)

- Get "unstuck" with techniques from a person who has been there.
- Learn effective delegating techniques and GET OFF OF THE TREADMILL.
- Create and develop systems and accountabilities for all aspects of the business.
- Create systems & processes documentation, and a dynamic operations manual.

- Learn time management for increased effectiveness and personal freedom.

BUSINESS ACQUISITION/START UP

- Choose the RIGHT business with our systematic approach to business startup/acquisition/franchise.
- Acquire capital with our proven resources and techniques.
- Have a "sounding board" as to feasibility of acquisition/start up.
- Create a practical business strategy/campaign that works!

BUSINESS TRANSITION (Exit)

- Learn how to groom the business for successful transition by creating INTRINSIC business value.
- Learn principles and techniques to employ in your business to attain maximum value when you exit.
- Learn transition modalities including employee sale, third party sale, and mergers.
- Exit your business in STYLE with a "GOLDEN PARACHUTE."
- Reduce taxation liabilities related to your business exit.

RESOURCES/CONNECTIONS AVAILABLE

- Sales and marketing support.

- Financial/ Accounting.
- Legal, Insurance, and Investment Professionals.
- Computer, IT, Website Development, Internet Marketing, SEO, Social Media Professionals.
- Business Brokerage and Franchise Search/ Placement.

Integrity Business Ventures, LLC
Centennial, CO 80016
Telephone: 303 739-5160
Fax 303 680-6450

Websites:
www.integritybusinesssolutions.com
www.integritybusinessventures.com
www.franchisepathstosuccess.com

Emails:
info@myIBV.com
info@integritybusinesssolutions.com

CPSIA information can be obtained
at www.ICGtesting.com
Printed in the USA
BVOW09s1704160418
513503BV00008B/164/P

9 781937 862671